I Am You

Visit www.booksurge.com to order additional copies.

I Am You

Craig Gilbert

I would like to thank all the members of the online forums that I belong to, as some of these poems would not have seen the light of day without them. Thank you for your faith, encouragement and unwavering support.

I would also like to thank Angela Harrison for producing the artwork for this book, which captures a lot of the themes contained in the poems herein.

Introduction

Welcome to I Am You, a unique collection of poems and musings that have been written to encompass my journey through life.

I have split the book into two sections: 'The Waking', which encompasses thoughts based on actual events and/or people, and 'The Dreaming', which is a more exploratory section, focusing on dreams and spiritual thoughts about life in general, although some of these poems have also been inspired by real people.

I would hope people who read these poems see and experience my journey from an innocent, young child right through to the man I am now, and take some sense of similarity to their own journey through life. I would also hope that through some of the struggles and less happy times I have endured, people can find some comfort and solace, especially if they are going through similar experiences. This is the whole reason why I have written these poems (as well as a personal enjoyment of course). I hope to make the reader's mind think of a time in their life, a moment when they experienced something similar to what I am putting down on paper, and to simply let them know that they are not alone with their feelings and emotions. We are all human, at the end of the day!

Of course, I cannot cover every human emotion or event; I can only cover what I, personally, have experienced. This is why I am sure this will not be my last book of poetry, and also why it is the third and not the first!

Thank you for reading this book, and for your interest. I hope you enjoy!

Craig Gilbert
March 2007

Table of Contents

Introduction   Page   vii

The Poems

PART ONE: THE WAKING   Page

Planets Part One   3
Planets Part Two   5
In The Glowing Sunlight   6
The Drums Echo On   8
The Piano   9
Haven   10
The Ridicule Of You   11
Blurry Vision   13
Waking Part One   14
Déjà Vu   15
Spoilt Like A Child   16
In The Cold Light Of Day   17
Waking Part Two   19
You Are Comfort   20
Scarf   21
I Am You   22
Softly   26
Waiting For The Year To End   27
The Pendulum Swings Through Darkness
      And Light   28
Mirrors   31
Damaged   32

The Longing Is Still The Same   33
Pink   34
Realm Of The Mirth   35
Shoulder   37
A Contemplation Of Tears   38
Love Lost   40
Mesmeric Imperfections   41
You Dance In My Shadows   43
The Sorcerer Of Muddle   46
A Sensuality Of Arms   47
Peanuts   49
When Energies Collide   50
Lost To The Immensities Of Anguish   52
Optimistic Life   54
The Inner Ending   55

Table Of Contents

PART TWO: THE DREAMING   Page

Through The Ley Lines   61
Weep At The Gates Of Nature's Spirit   63
Flowers   65
The Sad Can Dance   67
Gaia   68
Oblivion   71
The Nameless Fear   73
Synesthesia   75
Duet   77
I Often Dream I Am Running   79
Travel Through My Lenses   80
Warm Spirit In A Sea Of Cold Stone   81
Muse   82
Pale Hope In The Dream Beyond The Void   83
The Rapture   85
A Distance Of Minds (Collaboration with
     Karen James)   86
Making Peace   88
The Candle Flickers   89
Light Beyond The Shadows   90
Let The Wind Blow   92
The Vanishing   94
Demon In The Mirror   95
On The Edge Of Night   96
The One Spirit   97

Descent Into The Underworld   99
Body Blending   102
Introspection   104
Elemental   107
Temptress Of The Moon   108
Priestess Of The Sun   110
Darkness And Light (Collaboration with
     Panagiota Felecos)   112
Communion   115

PART ONE

The Waking

PLANETS—Part One

An empty void, not even the scent of oxygen –
Passes through the opaque blackness.
Cosmic swirls of particles form –
In the first sways of the first ever dance.
Guided by unknown forces,
It is enough to take one's breath away!
In awe, in fear, in delight –
A myriad of emotions burning at the core.

Thus are the planets born.
A fusion of energy and matter.
Creations of power and wonder.

Birth, and my eyes awake to a new world,
Blinking in the brilliance of the fierce light.
Although my mind cannot remember these
    images,
They are present, nonetheless.
Oxygen fuels my body,
Arriving out of the gloom with some speed,
To stop my life from ebbing.
With each breath I grow stronger,
My hands flexing against the air currents.

It is amazing to me,
That I know how to breathe,
How to see, smell, touch and taste.

Senses not yet nurtured fully,
But adapting immediately to my new
    surroundings.

The stars overhead shine downward,
The moonlight white and pure,
Bathing me in my innocence.

PLANETS—Part Two

How often it is I gaze at the stars,
Wondering about our place in the universe,
Feeling the cosmic rays burning into my soul.
So many delights in the heavens,
I am sure I will never see –
The distance is too far, I wager.
Yet I know they exist,
I can sense them, like a warm taste on my tongue.
Just when you think you've seen it all,
Something else comes along, and puts you in
      your place.

Now you are here,
And my eyes have opened again,
To the joys and splendours of this space.

My space.
My planet.

IN THE GLOWING SUNLIGHT

In the glowing sunlight,
I see you encompassed in darkness and fright,
A burden of chains hanging around your neck,
Dragging you down to the roots of this rotting
    deck.
I reach over to pick you up,
Lift you aloft like a small, long lost pup:
To simply bathe you in the warm sun's rays,
To let your cares and aches soothe away.

I wish it were this simple at times-
To hold you thus, wrap your arms around mine,
It would be such an easy task to achieve,
To caress you in glows of optimistic belief.
Oh such a life-affirming task,
To see you warm and safe as you bask
In the heat of nature's good,
Your woes and pain ebbing and slipping from
    your mood.

In the glowing sunlight,
Over here in this country of lakes and green
    delight,
I think of you, and wish good thoughts of you,
My heart beats in tune to commune you out of
    the blue!

I pray that this is enough
To reach you, across the ocean of dreams and
    rough
Waves that shatter against your shore,
Smashing like moments of grief against your
    core.

THE DRUMS ECHO ON

Boom, boom, boom...

This sound in my ears,
This deafening cascade of mental stimuli,
It batters at my mind's eye,
It halts the flow of sensation.

Touch.
My fingertips graze your shoulders,
So smooth and pale in the dim light.
I trace the curves of your splendour,
My nails brushing gently against your skin.

Feel.
Your aching flesh entwined to me thus,
I am focused on achieving the perfection:
The glorious fulfillment of both of our senses,
Captured in a fleeting moment of hidden
    fantasy.

Elsewhere.
This marvelous symmetry evades me.
To lose myself in the feeling,
Is all I require:
Yet why is it I hear the drums echo on?

THE PIANO

You played the piano with such talent,
Jazz chords and little dances of your fingers
Teasing the elegant white and black notes.
I sat beside you, trying to understand
How you made black blobs on a music sheet
Transform into a stunning performance of
    artistry.
Your patience, when I was at wit's end
Provided unparalleled wisdom;
Not just for the instrument,
Yet for other aspects of life itself.
I will always remember you,
An inspiration often at times when I was in pain
    -
Anguish at a love lost, fighting tears...
They all seemed to fall away,
Whenever we sat,
And played the piano.

*Dedicated to Kenneth Matthews, my teacher at
    the piano for many years.*

HAVEN

Come, nestle beside me,
Feel my heat entice thee,
Bring you out of your protective shell,
Embrace me and nurture me as well.
This haven is not just for you,
It is for us both to endure and become true,
Wrap me up in your precious arms,
Let us keep each other from harm,
Let our lust and our desires escalate,
Forget our minds and become soul mates.
Come, and fight the raging storms
That keep us both lost and forlorn,
Ignore what you think I am,
Seek out the real me and don't give a damn,
Believe in the way and what is just
Our lives have to entwine to survive, we must -
Journey towards a common goal,
Then, and only then, we will become whole.

THE RIDICULE OF YOU

I watch you from afar like a caring father,
Seeing your insecurities and nervous twitches,
Each idiosyncratic habit making me wince.
You remind me so much of myself,
A trembling figure in long corridors,
A shaky hand poking and digging at food -
With a fork that seems to have no control.
For an age I have tried to better myself,
To control such oddities and problems.
To an extent I have won,
I feel more a complete person,
Until I look at you,
And see me in you.
There is much to be done, still.
The ridicule of you,
Well, it not only relates to me,
Yet within it I can find a scrap of comfort,
That I'm not alone in my annoyances.
As I stand here, trembling, now,
Looking up at my future so solemnly,
I can see I am not such a freak -
A possessed demon existing;
I am much more than that.
I am so much more than that.
I am life eternal,
What comes through me comes through you,

Again and again and again,
As surely as stars burn and fizzle out -
We are part of the universe:
I will not ridicule you.

BLURRY VISION

Often, it is, how I walk
With blurry vision.

Blue eyes staring right past you,
Into a world of haze and mist!
It's not like I want to miss you -
I know you would embrace me,
Let me feel you are there -
Even if my sight fails me,
So why do I turn away?

Often, it is, how I walk
With blurry vision.

WAKING—Part One

I remember waking up from the dark,
Into a bright world of light and food,
My little feet running in new found expertise,
No other thought except for my stomach!

Simplicity itself…
How I envy such long lost days.

DÉJÀ VU

I seem to have been here before –
The aching, the pangs of the same loneliness
Threatening to overwhelm me in its iron grip.

I have lost my way,
I need to retrace my footsteps in the sand.
Try in vain to go back to higher ground,
Before the sea rushes to me,
And surges me away forever.

Time to make at least another stand,
Time for the days to drift by, but still time to
    mend.
I may be growing older.
I may not walk as fast as I did,
The sand becoming more sluggish beneath my
    tired feet,
Harder to walk through.
Yet I will walk nonetheless.

I will break free from the circle.
And soar!

Just takes a little time.

SPOILT LIKE A CHILD

So tender, so kind, you are to me-
Pampering to my every whim,
Obsessed with a cheeky desire
I know not how to react to you!
Love, I am not sure what this is-
To feel your passion envelop me,
Lasting over me, filling my lungs,
I am hopelessly lost in your feelings!
Kindness, I wish it was-
Each praise you bestow on me,
Attacks my well-being,
Chafes at my own soul,
Hatred comes unseen, not wanted
Into me, I don't want to feel like that-
Like a man who has a smaller soul than yours,
Demoted as you embrace and engulf me.

IN THE COLD LIGHT OF DAY

In the cold light of day,
My dreams, well, they just fade away.
Harsh stabs of white freeze
Assault my eyes, I tremble at the knees,
As I blink and look out into the piercing gloom
Of this, new, dark day, empty sky save for the
    moon:
A vacant circle of infinite mystery!
What lurks beyond I simply cannot see.
My life is so like that,
Filled with uncertainty, tit for tat.
I wonder if, once more,
I will fall, dissatisfied, alone on the floor,
No-one to stop me or come to my aid,
This, surely, is a world I have made.
My mind always puts up these boxes,
Tiny constructs in my brain, sneaky as foxes -
Blocking out any light handed to me,
Shielding those healing hands, stopping me
    being free.
I want to break out, I want to escape,
Find a new path in this tortured landscape.
Will you help me?
I fear not, although it could be your destiny:
Perhaps you will help me without my
    knowledge,

And I will find again that I have some courage.
It is then that I start once more to dream,
In the cold light of day, in the moon's harsh
    gleam.

WAKING—Part Two

I'm waiting for you:
To find me, to hug me, to love me.
Please fold me in your dreamy arms,
Smother me where I want to be smothered,
Fill me with the passion I sorely crave!

Please wake up, and see me.

YOU ARE COMFORT

You are comfort,
You are solace,
You are a haven amidst the decay.
You are the soil that nurtures the planet.
You are the soft pillow on my cheek.

I cast away all worry,
In a mere connection of moving feet,
A soft nudge from you,
The cares slip away like water droplets down
    my skin.

You are comfort,
You are solace.
You are a warm blanket around a cold person.
You are a shelter in a sea of storms.
You are the colour in a dark, grey day.

You are the gentle reason for my existence.

SCARF

I wear this scarf in memory of you,
This soft fabric of tartan-grey hue,
For it keeps me warm and cosy in the harsh
    winter's chill
And reminds me of your kindness, love and
    goodwill.

I never knew you as well as I should have done,
Only seeing you here and there when I was
    having fun –
Maybe on holiday or a fleeting visit to your home,
Yet I am your legacy, your blood, your flesh and
    bone.

So I wear this scarf in memory of you,
This soft fabric of tartan-grey hue,
Thank you!

It was yours once, for a while
Now I wear it fondly, and smile.

I AM YOU

Black.
It's the colour of you.
Dark, subtle and energising.
Often I lost you from view.
But you reappeared, special and new.

Friends.
It's what we are.
Knowing each other's intimate thoughts
Acceptance lived between us from afar.
No secrets destroyed us, nothing to mar.

Excitement.
My heart starts to pound
Just your voice was enough
When it sang to me I was bound
Mellifluous, it beckoned to me, such a
    crescendo of sound.

Trust.
Is what we had.
A deep sharing of entwined bonds.
No matter if I told you what made me sad
Or what delights I knew to make me glad.

Evolving.
Like a fine red wine
A maturity of self, a metal chain
Binding us so close, we entwined
You saw it all, you read the signs.

Love
Is what you gave to me.
And I reeled from the power of it
Part of me gave into your wisdom, things only
     you could see.
I was blind and foolish, when you wished it to be.

Passion
Is how we felt for each other.
It engulfed us in a fierce fire
A rapture of burning embers
Sparking off our bodies as we were lovers.

Thrills
Is what I remember feeling.
Cascades of dazzling energies
Flowing, ebbing and seeping.
As we explored, our bodies writhed in meeting.

Compassion
When either one of us suffered pain
We would shield, nurture and join the battle
To heal and ensure we survived, in the main
As one, we became sane.

Regret
Is how I feel now.
When the pain flowed and I left you
And I didn't speak, freeing you from your vow
Love, I hang my head and bow!

Anguish
Is what I received
Yet only after you had your own pernicious
    share
For then, what I had believed
Was proved false, and I grieved.

Hurt
This was the lowest ebb, the bottom
In our waves of emotion and life
I fell to the ground, my tears made the earth
    sodden
Reveries of times I missed, over but not forgotten.

Confusion.
And then, a spark!
A reversal of roles, so sudden, yet clear to me
As the sky gave way to the sun.

Belief.
A belief came to me
Of love, of loss, of sin
My blindness gone, I allow myself to see
What truly, truly can be!

Domination
You are the dominion in my world now
You bind me in chains of memories
Each link suffuses into my soul, I vow
Never to make mistakes, never to again fall and
  bow
To grovel at the dirt and mud
I am a man, I am strong.
I stand, and face you with no grudge
With passion, with need, with blood!

Soul mate
IS what you are to me.
You bind me as I bind you.
We are lovers, we are friends, we are one.
I am you.
I am you.

SOFTLY

I dream you...gently.
I love you...soothingly.
I kiss you...softly.
There is never any harshness
Certainly there was no intention of harm
The sadness of parting is real, but finite
The feather will blow sure and long in the wind
It will land again, somewhere further upstream
There, where it lands, the water will tinkle its
    fair music
The warmth will soothe our bodies and our
    aches.

Softly...there will be kisses.
Soothingly...there will be love.
Gently...we will dream.

WAITING FOR THE YEAR TO END

I'm just sat here,
Waiting for the year to end.
Thinking of you,
My new love,
Maybe *the* love.
My life is an ever increasing spiral,
A whirlpool of senses and emotions.
Who's to say what's around the corner?
It could be so much better for me –
Or so much worse.
Yet, I'm smiling –
Got to keep optimistic,
After all,
I am content!
I have you in my life now,
At the very worst, there will be happy
    memories.

THE PENDULUM SWINGS THROUGH DARK-NESS AND LIGHT

You won't see me again

Farewell to the country of my blinded yearning
I had longed for great happiness there
Tempted by skin, and flesh, and bone,
My allaying fears of being alone -
Suddenly it all becomes clear, and I am truly
    alone.

The pendulum swings through the darkness
    and light
There is nothing I can do or say
The fierce eternal black and the glow of intense
    bright
Encapsulated forever in a dance and sway.

I have fond memories of you both,
Especially of you, however, my love -
Yet was it love, that kept me in your arms,
Or simply my rising urgency of need,
The fact I never wanted to spend time
Like I had always spent it.

'Twas all a dream tinged in twilight.

The pendulum swings through the darkness
    and light,
There is nothing I can do or say,
The fierce eternal black and the glow of intense
    bright,
Encapsulated forever in a dance and sway.

Calm descends upon me and it is like I dwell in
    another world.
Mist and fog surrounds me, it is like I cannot see.
A soundless void with no screams or anger
    thrust upon me.
All I hear is my heart pounding.
Calling.
Calling.
Boom.
Boom.

Reaching out –

To someone I knew would answer the call.

There you were, the tears in your eyes,
Looking at me trying to forget
The way we were.
You succeeded beyond your own feelings,
You are not who you once were, but something
    greater.
There was me, all past forgotten, my journey
    returning full circle.
The suffering apparently all gone!

'Twas all a dream tinged in pale luminescence.

The pendulum swings through the darkness
    and light,
There is nothing I can do or say,
The fierce eternal black and the glow of intense
    bright,
Encapsulated forever in a dance and sway.

So now I follow my own journey,
My own path unravelling before me,
My pain and sorrow falling behind me,
Yet not forgotten.
Never forgotten.

You won't see me again.

MIRRORS

Open your eyes to the mirrors of life.
Lost souls walking in the fog at nine
The sea crashing to the shore in waves and
    ripples
I see this now as my ancestors saw it a
    millennia ago
I watch as tendrils of light pierce the gloom.
The fog sparkles incandescently, like thousands
    of
Tiny stars bouncing off each other.
Is this a trick of the light, or my own drunken
    sight?
Why am I walking here, at this time,
Along with those others who look like
They have no other place to go?
They reflect me.
They are mirrors of me.
We have all been here before.
I wonder how many people have taken this walk
At this strange time
And brooded on one's own soul?
I reflect them.
I am a mirror to them.
Yet mirrors can shatter.
Perhaps, it is time, to shatter mine.

DAMAGED

You do not know what you do.
You have no idea of the cruelty you bestow.
I wish I could lift my mood, escape the blue -
Thoughts that threaten to wash over me in
    their flow.
You do not physically twist a knife,
You do not forcibly hurl me aside,
Yet you are causing me strife!
Yet you are making my heart and mind collide.

You do not know what you do.
Someone so beautiful and alive
All that I've ever wanted is someone like you:
To share, laugh and simply confide.
You do not realize the pain caused to me,
You do not understand the feelings I've laden
    bare,
Yet you continue to inflict chaos in my sea -
The waves roaring higher and higher, sweeping
    me without a care.

It would be so easy to just leave,
To become a fleeting moment in the breeze!
Yet you know I am irrevocably damaged,
I will never leave while this inner ache is
    famished.

THE LONGING IS STILL THE SAME

There you are, once again, out of sight
Hidden beyond the far reaching horizons.
Each day comes and goes, without change.
Lately, I sit, each and every day,
Open to the possibility of us being one
Never giving up this vestige of hope,
Grabbing onto the desire that spurs me on.
It is a strange and menacing thing, at times,
Not to be dissuaded in any way,
Gathering strength and passion the more I wait.
I sometimes find I cannot breathe,
Sheer intensity as is my emotions,
Succumbing and possessing me,
Torturing me in the brutal, harsh fact:
I am still sat here, alone.
Longing for you to come through my door!
Luxurious thoughts, but I have them still.
Time after time, my mind goes in circles,
Here we go again, oh here we go again!
Echoes of days already gone by.
Something about you keeps me here,
Against all my sense and intelligence,
My body cannot move until you arrive,
Everlasting torment that only you can save me
    from.

PINK (Dedicated to Emma-Lou)

You are young and you love the colour of pink,
A bright shout at the world:
"Here I am, and here is where I belong"!

It is a statement for your ingenuity and
    boldness.

For as long as you can, I hope:
May you love the colour of pink.

REALM OF THE MIRTH

I'm dancing to an inner beat,
My core's despair replaced with tapping feet.
In the realm of the mirth
There is hope aplenty to unearth,
Hidden under every crevice and stone
Is a glee to be found, a joy to be known.
I often never find my way
To this realm of fun and sway,
In this world of damage and hurt,
It is hard not to fall beneath the dirt,
Mazes of challenges diverting your paths
Away from this place of merriment and laughs.
Yet for a small time I am finally here,
Wishing I could simply disappear:
Into this glowing realm of joyful dreams,
With flowing sun and rainbows of multi-
    coloured beams.

It is you who has brought me to this place,
Led me at last to this plateau of peace, laced
With the intoxicating virtues of all that is good
Dissolving all the anguish like a happy place
    should!
I must thank you for your assistance,
You are my deliverance
Into a land that seems giddily fair,

Where I can roam and laugh without a care.
I am sure this place is not meant to last,
Alas, I'm a realist, my fears rooted in the past,
Yet for a brief glimpse of time
This place is mine:
To share such a world with one such as you
Is enough for now, to perk my mood.
I am sure it could all end in a flash tomorrow
Yet for now I am content, and free from my
sorrow.

SHOULDER

I'll be your shoulder to cry on,
I'll be your saviour to call upon,
In the darkness of night,
When you are all alone and losing the fight.
I will embrace you in my arms,
Shower my love to you to keep you from harm,
For when the damage to you is done,
I will be here, where I belong.
Come and rest your weary head
On my shoulder, in my bed,
Feel my warmth surround you in glows,
Feel my heat soothe and caress your body
    blows.
You are bruised, hurt and feel so lost,
Let me be your guide and help you the most.
I want to be there for you no matter where we
    are,
No matter what journey we take or how far -
For at the end of it all,
I am your friend, your mind, your body, your
    soul.
In return you will provide for me
A place of inner peace and sanctuary.
You do not know my bliss
At helping you, sealed with a kiss.

A CONTEMPLATION OF TEARS

I am sad, tonight.
There is no real reason
For this passing tide,
Yet to you all
I will confide.

The weather is dark, cold,
Sinister gloom sweeping over
Grey houses and dusty windows.
The few, scarce orange pockets
Do nothing to light the moment,
Merely adding to the atmosphere
Of impending storms and shady walls.

I sit here alone, with sleepy shivers,
Tingling and heightening my senses,
Keeping me awake when
I would dearly love to fall to slumber,
To forget and forgive
The selfish motives of the ordinary,
The mundane and the dreary.

Thoughtfully scribing out words
Does seem to help my unwavering
Decay into the black state of depression,
Kind of a sharing of souls

When one's hand dances across the page,
Leaving marks of thought and feeling
For all to see.

So, why is it,
In this seepage of raw emotion,
That a lone tear cascades
In watery relief and silence,
Down my pale white face
To splatter as it does
Across the written page?

Perhaps this writing
Is not meant to last,
Yet merely to express the moment
Of one's own sadness.
How fitting it is, then,
That it is erased
By the physical formation of such emotion!

Let it be erased.
Let the feelings out.
I will feel better tomorrow,
My contemplation of tears is at an end.

LOVE LOST

I am love lost,
My mind seeping out soppy romanticisms
For someone who doesn't even know!
All others who show an interest
Are thrown aside without thought,
As my brain concentrates so hard on the one
That would make me eternally happy.
The mind is a fickle creature:
Even though I am hopelessly adrift,
Even though I am lost in a maze of heart,
There is still an exit to this accursed labyrinth.
Please, take my hand,
And guide me to my freedom.

MESMERIC IMPERFECTIONS

Once more, I need to end
What I have started:
A brief spark of untainted hope,
Despairingly crushed
Under a mountain of rocky reality.
I often despise myself
When these mesmeric imperfections
Come and hit me
With all their longing and lust.
At these times
I frequently wonder
That perhaps, this time,
This moment,
Will endure and last
Forever in a cascade of enchantment.
It is not meant to be, alas.
For here, I sit,
Writing these words,
Ending this belief once more.
It is a pain that I must capture
Over and over,
For ultimately I am helping you.
Now you can leave my web
Of corruption and acid -
That was so burning your
Body to violent dust...

You can seek a new path,
A new light of wisdom
To find the majestic soul
Who will return:
All your love,
All your angst,
All your fire,
All your hope -
In ways I just could not.

Forgive me, for my actions,
Forgive me, for my words.
In time,
I am hopeful,
That you will think back and thank me.

YOU DANCE IN MY SHADOWS

Shadows.

A smile brought me unto the world,
Under a sea of stars.
With the light came
The consciousness of humanity.

I remember those early days
Of dreaming and longing,
When I had no material interventions
To guide me away from my innocence.
I remember the little glimmers
Of sunshine on the grass,
The warmth that pierced through
The old, broken windows,
With the white paint
Peeling off.

Shadows.

A tear brought me unto loneliness,
My shattered dreams exploding
Like cold splinters of ice
As I sat in solitude.

I remember the futility
Of young, foolish hopes,
Dashed onto the rocks
Of the real solidity of the world.
I remember being told,
Unceremoniously,
To follow a normal path,
Flat and unending, each part
Made of the same
Type of brick.

Shadows.

A love brought me unto this country,
Hope and renewed vigour
Swatting away the dark nights
Like insects losing their bites.

I remember these few years,
Of fresh and invigorated mind,
Where the scenery dances
Before my brightened eyes,
Filling me with exuberance
And simple delight.
I remember the faces
Of those dear to me,
Sheltering me from harm's way
In a new world of enchanted energy.

Shadows.

You have brought me unto this joy.
Suddenly my hope and dreams
Are returned to me
Whence I thought them forever lost.

I will remember this time,
Your face, your eyes, your smile,
I will remember every touch,
Your whispers, your movements, your laughs,
For you dance in my shadows,
Play with them, and shape them,
Into something of your own creation,
And it soars through my soul !
Enlightening all that was once dissolved,
Banishing those old terrors from me.

I have a new lust for life.

THE SORCERER OF MUDDLE

The sorcerer of muddle,
He uses his skills to confound and befuddle!
Reaching his arms aloft,
He casts spells to alarm, to mock...
Those who are caught unaware,
Are caught in his lies, thus ensnared!
With mischievous peals of dark laughter
He conjures and moves without falter,
Quickening his pace as he seeks to lose
All your thoughts in a bewildered muse!
Run while you still can, with all your might,
This man can damage your soul with fright,
A flick of his fingertips and fire surges forth,
Enough to trap you in blind foolish thought...
Do not look into his fearsome gaze,
What you will see will hurt and amaze,
That, for every careless word his sorcery sparks
The glee in his eyes delves deep into his heart:

He knows not what he does,
He simply speaks about what he truly loves.
So when you next see the man of your fears,
Do not be too harsh on his mannerisms or tears,
He is always trying to find a way,
To reach you, to hold you in sway -
Not decay!

A SENSUALITY OF ARMS

With eyes transfixed, I watch thee,
An embodiment of sensation.
With heart trembling, I seek thee,
An enchantment of salvation.

You embrace me
In a sensuality of arms,
In a fierce wrapping of skin,
Sweat teasing and tingling:
My every crevice and contour,
Tingling my nerves such
Like they appear to be on fire,
Flames coursing through my veins,
As the heat laps at my body,
Licking me all over.

I embrace you back,
Our bodies threading together,
Spun from the same loom,
Merging and combining into
One colourful symbol of mother earth.
I feel your touch, sustenance,
The gentlest of forces
Yet somehow the most potent,
As I succumb to the feeling,
Lost unto the soil of birth.

Your moist, wet kisses,
Startle my neck,
As little trickles of water
Dribbles down my skin,
Like tears of warm glimmers,
Filling me with new life,
Sparkling in the beauty
Of all that is clear and pure,
Shimmering like lost pools
In the dry arid depths of my soul.

Breathe me into you,
Let us share the oxygen,
Dancing in sparks
Between our tongues.
I open myself to you,
To this new life,
Of feeling and nurturing,
My lungs fill with the glowing
Energies of love
And blossoming colours.

With hands locked tightly together,
We seek the physical delight.
With minds fused into one,
We seek the spiritual moment.

These are rituals that will span eternities.

PEANUTS

I remember the taste of peanuts,
Salty and nutty in my mouth,
Reminding me of happy times of long ago.
I always used to eat them
At Christmas, surrounded by family.
It is fitting, I think,
To remember such fun times,
When no-one thinks of their troubles,
Just revel in the party atmosphere
Of presents, food and silly television:
The snow falls outside.
The fireplace glows hot.
The tree shimmers in pale lights.
There is laughter and merriment.
Tomorrow,
I sense,
The troubles will come again.
Let them wait.
For now, I am content,
To sit here,
And nibble on peanuts.

WHEN ENERGIES COLLIDE

Even with my eyes closed,
I can see you.

Reach out, and embrace me fiercely.
I want to feel the glow from your soul
Warming through me and sensuously
Arousing and peaking and entwining
In the gentle sweetness of companionship.

As our energies swirl and collide,
Sparks fly from our bodies,
Inner heat derived from the source,
Our brilliance encapsulated and growing strong
In the lazy longings of romanticism.

Even with my eyes closed,
I can see you.

Let the energies mix.
It is time for us to soar.
Feel the love flow
From both of our hearts,
Nurturing the other in waves of pleasure.

I reach, and touch your hand,
Even though it isn't there:
Yet smile at the memory,
I feel the warmth surround me,
Envelop and soothingly bind me.

Even with my eyes closed,
I can see you.

LOST TO THE IMMENSITIES OF ANGUISH

Look how it is you fall:
The dark cloaks of despair
Clutching you in their talons,
Bringing you under,
Into a land where
All is barren and defeated.
Crushed, you have crumpled
Into the chasm of endless sorrow,
The blackness of the earth
Opening and dragging you in,
With a primeval force so strong
You cannot endure.

See how it is you lose:
Succumbing to this pit
Of harsh discord and detriment.
It is painful to my eyes as well,
As I see you plummet to your doom,
The beauty and glimmers that
Were once an angelic image of you -
Are now shattered into a thousand pieces,
To lay discarded and unwanted
On the scorched, dry land of emptiness.
The hurt encases you:
Suffocating and destroying your breath.

Is there any way out?

See how it is that I reach for you:
To pull you from the brink,
To stop you from becoming
Lost to the immensities of anguish!
Yet you are so far away,
So distant to me,
That my hand grabs at empty
Nebulous strands of air.
In my attempt, I fail,
And the tears flow from my lack
Of power, for I cannot save you,
Poor discontented spirit!

Regard me in your sorrowful countenance:
See how I too,
Am lost to the despair that sweeps around you,
For you engulf me in your waves of defeat -
Like a hand closing around my life energy,
Tightening, and then snuffing me out,
Leaving an empty husk where there was once
Light, harmony, and passion.
Embrace me, child.
Let our combined hearts flow as one,
To push back this black poison:
There may still be a chance before the end.

Is there any way out?

OPTIMISTIC LIFE

Mine is an optimistic life:
Shedding my worries and despair -
They have already moulded me, after all.
Sure, we learn from those dark,
Frightening moments,
The times when we are all alone,
The times when nobody seems to care,
The times when pain scorches the skin.
They are merely small pockets in the
Ocean of vast eternity -
Tiny barbs cutting into flesh and mind!
Yet merely lay your head back,
Let the waters of the Endless ripple
Around your tired shoulders -
Washing away the slivers of cold steel
That stab and wrestle with your heart.
For, with eyes closed,
The sound of gentle lapping at your ears,
Is enough to become one with the energy
Around you,
Soothing you,
Cleansing all your pores as decay
Drips away from your soul.

Loneliness is a state of mind.

THE INNER ENDING

Finally, I am here.

It has been many moons
Of sorrow, of neglect, of struggle,
It has been many comets
Of thunder, of fire, of passion,
It has been many suns
Of dawn, of dusk, of warmth,
It has been many stars
Of brightness, of light, of sparkles!

Yet now the end is here.
I've blown out the candle,
The wax has gone cold,
The darkness ensues,
And I am complete.

The silence is deafening.
I've cast out all my worries,
Put them in a mental box,
Discarded them like confetti,
Awakening to the new horizon.

My mind is free
Of all the stigmas
That so bound me to the earth
In torturous ways I could not
Endure...

I, of cursed thought,
Muddled by insatiable needs,
Lust and loves I could not kindle,
Oh, tearing at me,
Oh, cutting into me...

It is finally gone!
At last, I can see a new way home.

I am blessed indeed to have ones
Such as you around me,
To shelter and protect me
From the savage feeds
That reverberate in my brain.

You do, help me,
You shower me with affection
When I need it the most.
You do, inspire me,
To become better and less
Dwelling on my own
Tiresome thoughts.

So, it has come to this...
An inner ending,
A silent click of goodbye,
Without anyone knowing
Except me.
It feels good.
It feels liberating.

Finally, I am here.

It has been many moons
Of sorrow, of neglect, of struggle,
It has been many comets
Of thunder, of fire, of passion,
It has been many suns
Of dawn, of dusk, of warmth,
It has been many stars
Of brightness, of light, of sparkles!

PART TWO

The Dreaming

THROUGH THE LEY LINES

The seething and ripples of scratched sounds,
Of stone and of tree and of vision,
Echoes of the stillness eternal,
A cosmic array of new forces -
Yet guided by the ancient's knowledge,
Greets me and comes to my startled eyes
Like a momentary glimpse of enlightenment.
Palpable, I am ushered through the ley lines,
Travelling long and to far, mysterious places,
My beating heart shattering in my ears,
My mind adrift on a plateau of energy infinite.
The stars are pulsating and merging,
Faster and faster and faster,
They encompass all the glows of the heavens
In one mesmeric surge of enchantment.
I am soaring, made of nothing but star particles -
I have long since transcended a mortal's form:
I am now part of the flow,
Part of the cosmos,
The energy that binds the earth and the life.
It is at this point,
I see the meaning, the whole sweet melody
Of all that exists in the blend of the balance.
For a fleeting, powerful moment
I am encapsulated and made complete.

You are now my spirit.
You are now my soul.
Binding and entwining,
We lose ourselves from body,
We lose ourselves from thought,
We transcend and journey together,
Two feathers dancing and teasing at each other,
Tickles and sensations,
Merging with all the joy of a sunset's glow,
And the dawns of rebirth.

I feel this energy surround me,
In the stones, in the circles, in the lines,
This power is part of the land itself,
Not part of the decay and withering of time,
Something greater, indomitable,
A surge of euphoria sent back across the ages.
I embrace this sensual pleasure!
I embrace all that moulds and shapes me.
I embrace life in all its myriad of concoctions.
I have the spirit,
I have the nature,
Of all of life's creations.

I awake from the dream, so captivating,
A journey I long to take again...
Looking around at my world,
My life,
Perhaps I don't need to.

It is all here.

WEEP AT THE GATES OF NATURE'S SPIRIT

Cry into the deep, lush grass,
Share your bond with mother nature
In all its eternal majesty.

With the dark clouds fueling the sky,
The sinister bubbles of destructive forces,
The cries of slain animals and people,
The harsh reality that breeds greed and
    contempt,
The booming of weaponry and the sighs of
    chaos,
The toothless smile of a leering tyrant,
The shudder of the earth as it spins on its axis,
The death of goodness and of courage,
The endings of all that combined to make our
    life -
Oh let me weep!

In a rushed out embrace,
I take my soul on a new departure...
Trying to cleanse my body and all its macabre
    forms,
There must still be some compassion lurking
    somewhere.

I kiss the sodden ground,
I run my hands through the tall grass,
I luxuriate in the green glow of comfort,
I weep tears to water this new earth,
I weep at the gates of nature's spirit:
Embrace me and rip my body clean!
For underneath this deadly physical dwelling,
Beneath the cursed facade of ugliness,
Is a beautiful soul struggling to find sustenance...

You have come back to us, to change...

I am sorry for causing you pain.
I am sorry for all those who wreak havoc -
Those that burn and pillage and cause grief.
I am sorry for our souls
To be lost in the depths
Of hidden pools of darkness.
I am sorry for the damage untold,
The mocking laughter of our generations:
Voices shrieking into your beautiful skies.
Oh, let me weep!

So I cry,
Let out all the anguish foretold
In a billion voices -
I weep,
At the gates of nature's spirit,
Not just for myself, but for all of us:
There is still time to change our ways.

FLOWERS

I would send you flowers,
Tulips, roses and daffodils,
A myriad of colours to brighten your day,
If I knew you would accept them,
If I knew you would appreciate them.

I would send you cards and gifts,
For your birthday, Christmas, even deepest
    sympathies,
Anything to let you know I am here,
If I knew you would accept them,
If I knew you would appreciate them.

Often it is hard for me to know
Just how you feel about me -
Sure, I pine and harbour inner desires for you,
I would by lying if the gifts were just for you...
...yet my heart is right there with you,
Even in moments where I don't exist.

I would send you the world,
Mountains, rivers and forests,
A haven of sensual landscape,
If I knew you would accept them.
If I knew you would appreciate them.

I would send you the stars,
Planets, galaxies and the universe,
Space and time and all the meaning,
If I knew you would accept them.
If I knew you would appreciate them.

Often it is hard for me to know
Just how you feel about me -
My tiny globe in the sky.
I would be lying if I didn't want you to love me...
...yet my soul is right there with you,
Existing in all the fires and passions of the world.

Flowers, let the petals fall
And drift unassumingly across the barren skies...

THE SAD CAN DANCE

Sway, to the soft swirls of melody.
Dark chords stabbing at your lost soul,
Tearing at your heart with such tenacity,
Bringing back memories of those now gone.
It is like standing on the highest cliff -
A moment, and the sounds wrench you over,
The rush of the wind as you fall is
Oddly soothing
To your tired and weary eyes.
The moment you collide,
The impact of harsh clarity,
Jolts your being to the core,
Brings you back to the waking -
As the sounds grow loud and build on your ears.
You have fallen, but always another song,
To wrap you in warmth,
To pierce your soul.
Always another song...

GAIA

Mother earth, I am falling.

Like a dull ache throbbing against the wind:
A sense of something amiss, nebulous voices
    adrift,
Pounding, pulsating, an energy from the
    darkest core,
A swirling eddy, like a faint zephyr on a distant
    shore.

I can feel you.
You reach up through the very soil -
Sowing seeds of your victories,
Reaching out despite the decay and turmoil.
I breathe you in.
I want to breathe so deep.
You are my saviour, as I spin out of control,
My place winking out, as black as space,
No more energy burning amongst the stars.

Mother earth, I am falling.

Rent asunder, the storms beating against my
    brow:
Time crumbling away, religious chants surge
    and sway,
Rumbling, shuddering, a gap in the ancients'
    soul,
Crying out to be filled, to be reclaimed is its
    only goal.

I can feel you.
Your power entwines the sea and the trees -
Germinating glory of your new life,
Rising out of the terror, the clouded strife.

I breathe you in.
I want to breathe so deep.
You are my saviour, as I spin out of control,
My place winking out, as black as space,
No more energy burning amongst the stars.

Mother earth, I am falling.

But you will not let me crack -
Or burn in the dark flames of the ether.
There is a new beginning, a new life,
Inching out of the mud and dirt,
Bubbling beneath the deepest oceans:
For all that ends,
Is cradled to your loving breast.

Cradle me.
Become one.
Breathe new life.

OBLIVION

I want to see how dark it can get.

Journey, with me, now,
Into an ocean of sensual pleasure,
Faint kisses and murmured vows,
Swimming in waters, joined, together.

The waves of rhythm burst within my head,
Rocking my soul to the very core,
I thrust, and guide myself ever deeper, like I
    was in your bed,
Finding the irresistible wetness, that surge -
Of intense, warm shivers oozing from all pores.

Caress me in your wetness.
The feeling is all that I need,
To surge like the ebbs of the tide
Against your sweet miasma that is your body,
Slowly, gently, devouring you...
...eroding you...
...like waves crashing to a lover's shore.

Hands clutching shoulders,
Face and tongue lapping in the neck,
Each crevice and contour painstakingly revered...
...oh my love, kiss me!
Embrace this mortal soul.
Push and thrust in time,
Let us ride and journey ever higher,
To another plane—another reality
Of melting tears and pools of hot sweat,
Fiery friction and sapping strength...

I want to see how dark it can get.

Journey, forever, with me now,
Into this world of sinful pleasure,
Eager kisses and shouted vows
Swimming in fires, burned, together.

THE NAMELESS FEAR

I sit in the darkened room,
Eyes trying to pierce the descending gloom.
Shivering uncontrollably in the cold sliver of
    dark -
Trying to fathom why we are so distant and
    apart.

My mind analyzes as my eyes view my naked
    form,
Goosebumps tingling the flesh as I sit alone.
I hug myself, trying to grab a shadow of
    warmth -
Yet the light and hope has ebbed from the
    hearth.

'Twas once a happy place, this,
Filled with laughter and mutual bliss,
'Twas once a place of music and song,
A dwelling we sought to keep in our hearts,
    now gone.

So I sit, here, alone and naked in the cold,
Trying to piece together how I came to be here,
    so bold.
Why it is that you are not here,
Why my mind shrieks in a nameless fear.

My hands outstretched, reaching out...
My body reacts, praying to the devout...
Come back and rescue me....
Come back and fill me with glee...

The dream is a strong one,
It floods my veins, sinew and bone.
Encapsulate me in a warmth only you can
    achieve,
Nurture me in a cloak of your love and make
    me believe.

SYNESTHESIA

Like a train on the track;
In rhythmic waves in my mind:
I sense tunnels, and lights, and colours -
A body journey, feet tapping
In tune, in connection with the sounds.

I so want to help people,
See them shed their fears and worries -
Lose their lack of confidence -
I so want to see them smile,
Confide in me and travel on my journeys.

Like a boat sweeping through the sea;
Pulsating senses rock my body:
I see the water, the sun shimmering, the
    moonlight -
All at once, a blaze of passionate colour
In perfect connection and contemplation.

I see you so sad, tears flowing,
I reach out, and touch your hand -
So sweetly, so genuinely, so understanding -
I want to brush those tears away,
Take you in my arms and encompass you in
    love.

Like a plane gliding effortlessly in the twilight;
The throbbing roar of the engines:
I float in the air with angelic wings -
Soaring aloft, heading for the stars
My soul perfectly aligned with the heavens.

I so want to soothe and calm,
Make others feel this euphoria I sometimes
    have -
Bathe all in a wondrous radiance -
Yet the journey ends, my wings disappear
And I am human, once more.

DUET

He wonders where she is -
What she is doing, as he thinks:
Is she reading a book?
Or laughing with someone new with a happy
    look?
He drinks some red wine -
Wonders if she likes the same tastes so fine:
Is she sitting down to a romantic meal?
Or kissing with someone new with passionate
    zeal?
His heart longs for her love -
He prays for someone to listen, anyone above:
Does she pray like he does?
Or is there someone new she now loves?

She wonders where he is -
What he is doing, as she thinks:
Is he walking in the sun?
Hand in hand, maybe, with someone fun?
She sips at her glass of water -
Wonders if her love so distant will falter:
Is he now gone away forever more?
With someone new, his feelings no longer at war?
Her heart yearns for her one -
She prays that he hasn't gone:
Does he pray like she does?
Or is there someone new he now loves?

Fate twists and turns, we can never tell,
Which way it will go, bad or well,
I am hopeful that one day I will clearly see -
That my one true love will come for me.
Wait for me, I will wait for you.
Forgive me, I will forgive you too.
Capture my heart, I will capture yours -
Let our fires burn down all the doors.

I OFTEN DREAM I AM RUNNING

I often dream I am running,
At times it can be of slow motion,
My arms and legs pumping but getting
    nowhere,
Other times the universe zooms past me,
A cacophony of noise and swirls,
Lights so alive they make sound,
A surge of speed as the images fly by.

I often dream of such things,
I often wonder what this all means.
Am I rushing, blindly, in my own life?
Or am I just letting time slip by,
Without a word or a care?

Just my legs moving,
Running, faster, and faster, and faster,
Building up to a frenzied, dizziness of limbs.
Often I trip, stumbling over my own feet
To fall into a sea of nightmares.

It is fitting I can still wake up after these visions.

Always time to run.
Always time to change.

TRAVEL THROUGH MY LENSES

Travel through my lenses
Roam and see through my eyes
Awake to all that surrounds me
Vestiges, shadows and demons!
Evil stirring around every corner,
Lords of doom come to greet me, gloating:
They know one of their own...
Hope strangled and cast asunder,
Rights and wrongs merging into obscurity
Obsessive thoughts spinning around my soul,
Urging me to act in ways I do not want to,
Goading me into being something I am not,
Hurting me in their twisted body and mind
    games.
My soul despairs from it,
Yearns to escape, to evade the devilish horde!
Look through my cracked lenses
Envelop me with your wisdom and light,
Nurture and tend to my wounds -
Show me the path I need to travel,
Ease me back from the brink!
Save me, my love, from the growing darkness.

WARM SPIRIT IN A SEA OF COLD STONE

Warm spirit in a sea of cold stone,
Caress me and smother me and bring me home
To the time of intoxication and a scene that is
    merry,
Bring me to the sunny laughing harbour by ferry!

Your soul is enriched with happiness and laughter
It is your inspiration with that lust for life that
    I'm after
Dance and squeal, shimmer and grow bright
In this chaotic world I will show you no fight.

You light my world with intensity never seen,
Guiding my way to the places that are green
The sun beating down as we dance in the wild
Our amusement and delight is far from being
    mild.

Warm spirit in a sea of cold stone,
Caress me and smother me and bring me home
For your jokes and laughter are joys to my ears
So long as I am beside you I will have no fears.

MUSE

Intoxicating soul,
I breathe you through my eyes and ears.
Inspiring heart,
I nurture you through my mind and blood.
Those sweet ways of you,
Those dark images of you,
The powerful mystique surrounding you,
All are golden to my thoughts and desires.
At times all I think of is you,
Your passions and lusts apparent to me
As they are to you.
My muse, breathe me in,
Through your own eyes and ears.
My muse, nurture me,
Through your own mind and blood.
At times I think we are one person
Simply split into two,
Trying to find the other part.

PALE HOPE IN THE DREAM BEYOND THE VOID

I have often dreamed of one like you.
A gleam of pale sunshine breaking the dark
    clouds of grey,
A shimmering across a vast ocean of blue,
A thought of warmth and heat, hints of light to
    show the way.
I have often journeyed far for one such as you,
A quest took willingly, to blossom and feed my
    soul,
For when at last all is complete and you are in
    view,
I know I will have returned to stable ground,
    never to fall.
You are a metaphor for all that is good and
    sweet,
My mind's eye burns aflame to gaze upon you.
To behold your physical form, from your head
    to your feet,
It would light a beacon of immense feelings in
    me, all anew.

Would you take me in your arms and let us entwine?
Would you embrace and kiss me and flow from me
so fine?
Become one, a mutual sharing of bodies and mind
To gush like liquid across ground and flesh,
revitalising in kind?

I see you smile, a hidden thought playful within
you.
I am sucked into the void that is beyond your
emerald eyes,
Wanting to smile and share the feelings, my
darkness to be destroyed right through,
To give myself to you, to feel the ecstasies and
the joyous cries.
I have often dreamed of one like you.
There, within that pale hope in the dream
beyond the void, out of sight,
Behind all the emptiness and clouds, across the
ocean of blue,
You will exist, and shatter the ties of discord,
and the endless night.

THE RAPTURE

My eyes shine when they see the beauty,
A word of superficial sophistication.
My lips curl and smile when I see the curves,
Small lines undulated by firm muscle and flesh.
My nose breathes deep when it smells the scent,
Pheromones and aphrodisiacs playing with
    sensual awareness.
My ears listen to the gentle, sweet caress of the
    voice,
Slight inflections in sound enough to tingle.

All encompassing, these senses, delighting in
Blissful ignorance:
Of a soul, of a mind, of a heart.
I am ensnared thus!
Trapped and bound by the essence of the
    surface.

A DISTANCE OF MINDS (Collaboration with Karen James)

Away, across the ocean of azure dreams,
I sense a soul, bright and alluring,
Sending me light,
Coruscating across the water in beams!
Making me almost see you in fantastic shades,
Greens, and reds, and violets, soothing,
Ending the long darkness of night.

Across the seas, he beckons me
our souls move through moonlit waves of blue
scintillating light though the night
brilliant illumination invites ~ lures him in
what does he see, can he really see me for me
not locked up images of a goddess that only exists
    in fantasy
sadly, my reality will never be all he dreams
my blacks and blues that are always hued
my darkness that forever shadows light
please, oh, please my heart ignite

Will I take this long, arduous journey?
Travel and fly like a bird to see you -
The idea certainly has crossed my mind,
Or will I wait, in quiet and relaxed anticipation,
For you to visit me, and pass the light -
From your own sensual body to mine,
Bathing us both in fierce red glows of delight!

Another universe in the cosmic sky
A comet that burns in my minds eye
Give me wings so I can fly
that million mile to touch his smile
Bestow my love and shower grace
Take my hands
Caress his face
If only wings my arms could be
I'd fly him love across the seas

Through your eyes I see my soul,
Stretching out across time and the ether
Our bodies are melting and fusing into one
    whole -
A new beginning, a new emotion, something raw
Touching us like effervescent bubbles,
Exfoliating our skins as fresh and as vibrant -
As if we dipped ourselves into clear, calming water.

In my eyes what does he see
Passion that burns inside of me
reflecting bodies in waves of flesh
hearts that beat as one
they mesh
The passion of our souls embrace
Nothing transcends time and space
One touch perhaps could make me see
a spark
it's love
we're meant to be.

MAKING PEACE

I don't want to fight anymore.

To all the people I have ever met,
Tears shed of sorrow and regret
Pain caused and received in winter's snow
The shock and trauma felt in the afterglow.
I want to make peace with you all,
No matter how insignificant our interaction, big
    or small,
Whether it be the split of a doomed lover's heart,
Or harsh words spat in anger driving men apart
I forgive all who despise me or think me mean,
As I forgive them from petty squabbles and
    fabric torn at the seam.
Many of you I will never see again,
Yet it is difficult for me to refrain
From thinking of you as part of my crazy past
Each of you has changed me, each better than
    the last.
Let us all make peace, for time doth run short,
And before spirit's end I will not be caught.

THE CANDLE FLICKERS

The candle flickers
As if it represents my shifting mind.
Endless thoughts circling
Often like dark, black clouds.
Making the light dim and
The cold beckon.

Yet the light flares again,
Warming and burning though the mad cravings
The dangerous desires, the thoughts that really
    shouldn't be there
Burn, burn, strong and true
Burn, burn, strong and true
My heart yearns for improvement
It yearns for the light.
Tomorrow is a new day
And I am thankful for that.

LIGHT BEYOND THE SHADOWS

In excitement, the thrill of it
Enough to urge my startled mind to sit
Up and take notice of you.
Seductive whispers beckon me to a side,
A part of me often buried and deep.
The thrill of it fills my core
The mind thinks of nothing else but the rapture
Before I can control this I am hopelessly lost
To you, my darkness.
Afterward there is guilt,
A worry that I am transforming into
Something alien, something devilish.
I dare not do this again,
Seductive whispers guide me to the black
    pools of your desire
And I am startled once more.
Oh Lord—forgive me for this—help me stop!
I want to be better than this.
You are my darkness,
Yet I need the light evermore.
There you are, my fire, my nurturing goodness.
Come to me,
Entwine with me
Let us share a union of immensity
Cutting away the dark
Stripping it down

To the light beyond the shadows.
I want to stay here
In the light beyond the shadows.
I know you will help me.

LET THE WIND BLOW

Let the wind blow and rustle the leaves.
Let the breeze swirl and caress my face.
Signs of life and movement,
Tantalising me when I think there is nothing.
For days now I have been struck,
In a senseless and miserable rut!
My world seems to have stood still,
Despite hopes that tomorrow will at least bring
    something.

Monotony, that's what I've stumbled into.
A lack of passion, of dreams, of lust,
Signs of decay and of boredom.
I must do something.
Anything, to break free of this lapse in my
    journey.

So the wind blows.
I follow it to the sea.
Looking at the waves crashing onto sandy
    pebbles.
Foam and salt hissing and seething.
Part of me wants the foam to envelop me,
Cover me and make me escape.
Part of me wants to dance and frolic in the
    waves,

To feel the onslaught of freezing water,
To wake me up from this reverie.
Part of me wishes you were here.
A hiss, and the waves recede.

Let the wind blow, and rustle the leaves.
Let the breeze swirl and caress my face.
I feel you on the wind.
My passion, my dreams, my lust,
Tantalising me when I think there is nothing.

THE VANISHING

Here I am now, filled with glorious memories.
Here I am now, engulfed in harsh regrets.
This life has taken many turns.
This life has taken many forms.

In the soft wink of a tear-filled eye,
I feel better, my heart's burden ebbing,
All the hate, depravity and senselessness
Gone in a pool of turquoise water,
Winding its way down my cheek.

Vanish, and be done!
Forgive and forget events buried in history.
Shine, clean up and move on.

I wipe away the water on my face,
My eyes blink and look forward
To a learned, beautiful horizon.

Here I am now.
Here I am now!
Take me, embrace me, world,
Carve me out of stone,
For I am better!
It is time to come home.

DEMON IN THE MIRROR

I see you.
Looking at me.
Your malevolence,
Your enmity,
Oozing outward to envelop me.
Be gone, for I don't want you here,
In my life—ever!
Yet you take great mirth,
In popping up when I least expect it,
To tarnish and damage my soul.
Your claws dig into my flesh,
Hurting and drawing my life's blood,
And you cackle in evil glee,
Gloating at my new misfortunes.
Demon in the mirror,
Leave me, now,
Let me be,
Let me control my own destiny
Without your laughter echoing in my ears.
Why do you always return to haunt me?
Catching me, always,
At my lonely moments.

ON THE EDGE OF NIGHT

I am black.
Darkness descends
And you cannot see me.
I am part of the flowing edge of night.
Gothic eternal,
Part of the menace and sinister forces
Of the insurmountable gloom.
Occasionally,
You may catch a fleeting glimpse
Of me running, or moving
Rapidly through the shadows,
A vain attempt,
Possibly,
To bring myself out of the murk!
Yet I am soon lost once more,
Swallowed up by the dark
Entity that binds us all -
Engulfing us in never ending
Throes of despair.

THE ONE SPIRIT

Where did you come from, my love...
Arriving as you did in an explosion of strident
    sound
Amidst the elemental tempest that raged
Around us?

Just as I was about to get lifted away:
Ripped asunder by these vast inner storms -
Turmoil surrounding and blackening my heart,
Emotions of despair intruding on my sanity...
Your being appeared just in time to save me.

Oh, you were so full of life and joy!
Laughing in a playful manner so becoming;
Your infectious soul imposing upon my own,
Stamping its authority and sprinkling light
On my opaque, impenetrable darkness!

This aura of brightness envelops you,
And indeed all those whom you touch;
Your fingertips exude such sensuality
And gentle caress, tantalizing -
Like motes of energy striking and coalescing.

I gaze into your pools of deep sincerity,
Locked and fallen into their mysterious depths:
Right there and then I feel a warm glow
Spreading through me and energizing me -
I am transfixed on your form and spirit.

My wish then transcends all others,
Destroying all the eddies of unquiet and despair,
Serenely filling my being in newfound glory:
Quite simply, I want to become one
With the spirit so amazing before me.

Where did you come from, my love...
Arriving as you did, as an angel sent to me
In my time of need and sorrow?
Amidst all this violent energy
That curses and scoffs at us?

The one spirit.
It comes for us all.
When we need it the most.

DESCENT INTO THE UNDERWORLD

I walk along a misty path,
Trees appearing silently out of the gloom ,
Muffled by white mystery and odd winds.
My heart quickens in pace
As I walk faster -
To be walking here alone
Is tantamount to lunacy.
Out of sight, I hear strange voices,
Guttural, not even human;
More of an untamed, wild beast -
My mind imagines all kinds
Of unfathomable monsters.

There are stone steps suddenly
In front of me.
I descend, down into the blackness
Of the caverns below.
Torches flicker unceremoniously
Lighting my way
In lights that dance and create
Muddled thoughts in my mind.
The cold seeps around my body
Like it is alive, talons of ice
Clutching me in an iron vice!
I dare not tarry.

I must rush,
Urge my body to move faster...
Deeper down the stone steps,
They spiral and spiral and spiral,
Looping around my soul
In coils of unrelenting fear.
Behind me, I hear cries,
Just as I do to my sides,
And to my front,
As if I were part
Of a huge nest of
Living creatures.

Then,
So slowly,
The throbbing pulse of a hum,
The sound of an ancient, intricate machine,
Powering up
The depths of this darkness,
Belching in the stomach
Of blackness,
Breathing the hiss of life
To this unnatural world.
Ever increasing is this noise
As I finally reach the end of the steps.

Before me I see a vast array
Of pipes, and machinery,
A greasy network of metal.
As I walk through,
Engines and pulleys are moving,
Sinister echoes drift
Through my heightened senses.
I need to get away from this place
Before my heart gives way
And explodes in fear in my throat.
I must get out!
I must get out!

Frantically, I run towards
What I can see -
A doorway, with a halo of light:
Silhouetted amongst the darkness.
I feel claws on my skin,
I hear grinding of inhuman teeth,
Reaching out
To grab me, to use me
For food and for sustenance.
With a final despairing effort
I lunge through the door
And my eyes are startled to see the image:

My bedroom.

BODY BLENDING

Body blending,
Mending:
That inner core of seduction.

Hearts beating,
Meeting:
A sense of blissful infatuation.

Entwined skin,
Bring:
The euphoria of sweaty carnality.

Tongues locked,
Rocked:
To the rhythm of the kiss.

Savage primal,
Spiral:
To the surge of the lusting.

Flesh heat,
Meet:
Become one with the energies.

Souls entwined,
Find:
That which means the most.

Body blending,
Mending:
That inner core of seduction.

INTROSPECTION

Yet again I look inward,
To see my mortal soul.
Bared for all to see:
My fears and anxieties.

Strip down the layers
of this skin,
Sharpen those claws
To peel back the fabric of what lies within.

What do you see?

Do you see yourself,
Locked in hidden fantasies,
Or do you see a monster -
Shrieking in the wind
Of vast eternal forces,
Mustering strength
To cry out
Against all the hatred
And passions of this world?
Or do you sense the same thoughts:
Drifting from my mouth to yours
On a plane of insecurity?

Look beyond the skin.
Look beyond the flesh and bone.
Tear me apart with your eyes,
Feel the warmth and share the soul.

Pierce into the gloomy
Facade of my pain,
Behind the cries of torture
That we all scream in unison.

What do you see?

Do you see your heaven,
Floating in the azure sky of creation,
Or do you see your hell:
A screeching of demonic voices
Burning with power in the night,
Mustering death
To destroy
All that is weak and lost
In these tiny pockets of humanity?
Or do you sense the same thoughts:
Inexorable in their travel,
From your body to mine?

Look at me.
Feel me.
Kiss me.
Hug me.

Know me.
Capture me.
Become me.
Deliver me.

In the end,
It's all
A calm, intelligent
introspection of equality.

ELEMENTAL

From the hidden dusk
I see the orange flicker,
Red passion igniting the cold:
Energy of exploding planets.

Warm floods of molten lava
Attack and mould the world
Tamed only by the fury
Exerted by the stormy skies
Raining down in droplets of pureness.

Energy that binds us all
Asserts and engulfs us,
Reactions to the shaping universe
Time hardens and cools the soil
Hones the mountainous landscapes.

Arriving at last, we come,
In hurls of energized matter,
Real star stuff spread from the source.

TEMPTRESS OF THE MOON

There you are, bathed in eternal glows,
The silver basking your sensual form,
Tracing the contours of your skin, so maddeningly
To my eyes, as I drink in your view.

What are you trying to achieve...
With those sultry looks and hidden gleams?
The truth lies hidden, beneath your stares,
That bore into me and rip me to shreds.

I have no secrets left to hide from you,
For you have gleaned them all from my soul,
Pulling them out of me as if you
Were pulling a blade of grass out of the soil...

...crushing it betwixt your fingers.

Yet I am drawn to you,
Like metal to a magnet,
Stuck to your pristine allure,
Transfixed and locked in your webs.

What are you trying to achieve...
Keeping me like this in a state of limbo?
Trapping my form and mind to yours,
Not giving me unique thought, merely all yours?

The moon rises high, silver and shimmering
As you flick your hair back, making it flow
Behind you, like a hidden stream of secrets,
Full of dangerous intrigues and beauty.

It is all a game to you, I feel,
As you harness the powers of the stars and
    moon,
Encircling this life in powers of night,
Of darkness and forbidden pleasures...

...these chains grow ever tighter around me.

PRIESTESS OF THE SUN

There you are, captured in warmth,
That brightness that encapsulates you
And embraces me
In a glimmering of eternal sunlight.

What is it that you want to achieve?
When you look at me with those green
Emeralds of scintillating energy and endless
    beauty -
Playful features and soft sensuality.

You envelop me thus,
Encasing me in a heat of shedding skin,
Pouring yourself down into me,
Sharing and engulfing me in flames...

...I succumb and burn in your embers.

The sun rises high in the pale blue,
The land is healed and glows eternal,
Your arms and hands reach for the sky,
Touching the light and bringing it down to you.

It is then, I wonder about you,
When you are so beautiful and full
Of the circle of pristine clarity,
Clean and vibrant under the pure sunshine...

...I hear birdsong and I marvel at your beauty.

DARKNESS AND LIGHT (Collaboration with Panagiota Felecos)

Oh, scorched earth,
Open and drag me down into you -
End this melancholic torment!
For years I have been struggling on,
Nothing to my name and nothing in my world:
I am bitter at this charred, barren land,
I am angry at these violent surges of storms -
That we have somehow created, you and I.
Oh, lost and shattered world,
Open and drag me down into you.

Oh my lost wandering child,
Let me bathe you in my rays of Light.
Let me ease your struggles and torment,
For the earth shall rejuvenate itself as it always
    does.
Do not be bitter, for this land will not remain
    barren,
And the storms shall cease.
Bask in my beams of warmth and
Feel me envelop you with loving care,
For you are not alone.

Oh, fleeting moment,
You cause me great turmoil and sorrow.
I am lonely, surrounded in husks of emptiness.
What once showed great promise
Has turned to dust and ash -
Sour and bitter on my tongue.
No matter how hard I try to reach you,
I am battered backwards by waves of
Distance and malcontent.
Oh, lost and broken promise,
Engulf me and burn me to ash.

Oh wounded soul,
You are not destined to be alone
In your sorrow and emptiness.
Feel my warm embrace as I gather you close to
    me,
As the distance begins to dissolve.
Let me soothe away your malcontent.
For out of the ash, hope will rise and be born
    again
Like the coming of a new dawn,
With the promise of a better tomorrow.

Oh savage fury,
Unite and overwhelm me in your destructions.
Hurtle me into the blinding void of emptiness
    and of pain,
Across the ethereal skies of disturbance.
Envelop me in your harshness,
And rip me asunder as a
Sacrifice for all the despair our race has
Bestowed upon thee!
I do not belong in your perfect world.

Oh lamentable one,
Do not be overwhelmed by emptiness and
    pain,
Do not succumb to the despair.
Your sacrifice is not what I seek,
For I hold no fury against you my precious one.
Let my atmosphere of love and light be the
Balm to the wounds you have sustained,
And fill up the void within.
For what was once broken, shall be made
    whole again.
Out of darkness, light shall rise.
Out of despair, hope shall flourish.
Come to me and I shall embrace thee, you
    belong,
For without you, I am nothing

COMMUNION

I rise and stand
For the first time,
An echo of everyone
Who stood before me.
I run through the grass
Savouring the warmth of the sun,
A new person in the crowd
Joining all who have walked here.
I sense the linkages
Of all history and time,
Spread out before me,
Passed down in legacy.
It is fitting to be part
Of the new future,
The new cycle of
Generation and dreams.
I walk this path,
New and exciting to me,
Just as you have all done before,
Looking at the same scenery.
I taste this new air,
Breathing in delicately
My lungs sharing the same
Sensation as all of you.
There is an intimacy here,
Of all that surrounds us,
Is shared by all of us,
It is a cascade of entwined

Emotions,
They run through me,
As they run through you.
The times of hate,
Of fear, of despair,
Are burdens we all
Have to face,
In singular, unique forms
Related only to one's own circumstance.
Yet these bitter,
Harsh pills of discord,
We all bite into,
Swallowing them often:

And we think we are alone.
The truth behind this world,
These thoughts and images,
Is that we are never alone,
We are caught in the same web
Of all life before and after.
It is something to cherish,
And value, in time of grief -
The one solace,
I hope and crave,
Is that the learning comes
Dwindling our pain,
Slowly, inexorably,
We will become new,
Fresh,
Spirits of sense and love.

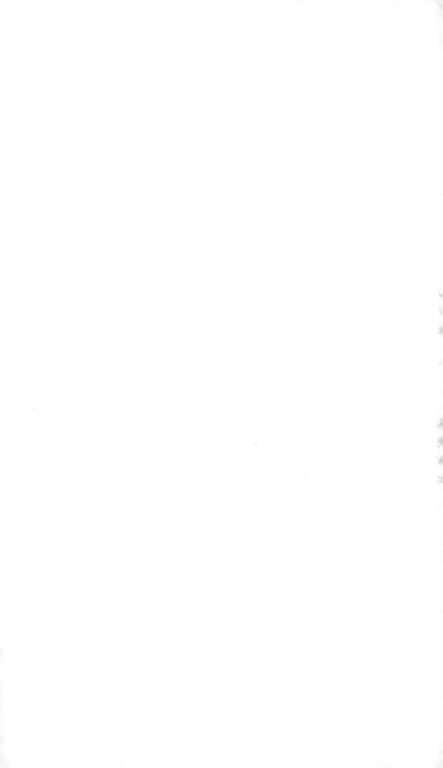

6349406R0

Made in the USA
Charleston, SC
14 October 2010